"...But I only had 2 beers"
Truth Talk from over 25 Drunk Driving Lawyers

by Richard Jacobs

Disclaimer

This book does not offer nor contain legal advice. All of the information provided is purely informational, and you, as the reader, must NEVER rely upon it without seeking qualified legal counsel. Laws differ by state, county, jurisdiction, year, and are subject to change any time, with or without notice.

The author, all contributing attorneys, and everyone involved with this publication specifically disclaim any responsibility or liability for your use or lack of use of this information. If you are facing a criminal charge, have previously faced one, or in the future face one, take note that this publication must never take the place of consulting with an attorney who knows the particular laws involved in your situation.

Purchasing, reading or using any of the information contained in this book does not constitute nor imply an attorney-client relationship with its author, editors or any of the attorneys who have contributed to the book.

CONTRIBUTORS

Richard Jacobs - Primary author & editor

Jennifer McKnight - Technical editor

Attorney Kevin Leckerman (Philadelphia, Pennsylvania & Southern New Jersey) - Contributor

Attorney Mark Taiani (Pittsburgh, Pennsylvania) - Contributor (Watch his interview: http://goo.gl/FeSuI)

Attorney Ken Stover (Reno, Nevada) - Contributor (Watch his interview: http://goo.gl/p49iu)

Attorney Zach Westerfield (Denver, Colorado) - Contributor (Watch his interview: http://goo.gl/30bok)

Attorney Anthony Lowenstein (San Francisco, California) - Contributor (Watch his interview: http://goo.gl/qgcEP)

Attorney Justin Summary (Saint Louis, Missouri) - Contributor (Watch his interview: http://goo.gl/UHcdO)

Attorney Brendan Kelly (Omaha, Nebraska) - Contributor (Watch his interview: http://goo.gl/rCMtO)

Attorney Joshua Hale (San Diego, California) - Contributor (Watch his interview: http://goo.gl/H9EtV)

CONTRIBUTORS

Attorney John English (Lansing, Michigan) – Contributor (Watch his interview: http://goo.gl/MmpwL)

Attorney Michael Byrne (Chicago, Illinois) – Contributor (Watch his interview: http://goo.gl/qKQwb)

Attorney Shannon Wilson (Portland, Oregon) – Contributor (Watch her interview: http://goo.gl/cxeA0)

Attorney Jeff Yeh (Los Angeles, California) – Contributor (Watch his interview: http://goo.gl/qugWJ)

Attorney Kavan Grover (Atlanta, Georgia) – Contributor (Watch his interview: http://goo.gl/LzimE)

Attorney Lawrence Wolf (Los Angeles, California) – Contributor (Watch his interview: http://goo.gl/Hxjp0)

Attorney Dale Naticchia (Cleveland, Ohio) – Contributor (Watch his interview: http://goo.gl/BIPI0)

Attorney Doug Riddell (Dayton, Ohio) – Contributor (Watch his interview: http://goo.gl/RcEIi)

Attorney Steve Litz (Monrovia, Indiana) – Contributor (Watch his interview: http://goo.gl/shbKu)

CONTRIBUTORS

Attorney Aaron Bortel (San Francisco, California) – Contributor (Watch his interview: http://goo.gl/E2VQD)

Attorney Michael Tillotson (Virginia Beach, Virginia) – Contributor (Watch his interview: http://goo.gl/srz6z)

Attorney Fred Woods (Greenville, South Carolina) – Contributor (Watch his interview: http://goo.gl/qy4z6)

Attorney Steven R. Tinsley (Orlando, Florida) – Contributor (Watch his interview: http://goo.gl/MNfwK)

Attorney Stuart Collis (Ypsilanti, Michigan) – Contributor (Watch his interview: http://goo.gl/N3hmr)

Attorney Carl Spector (Fair Lawn, New Jersey & New York, New York) (Watch his interview: http://goo.gl/dkYhs)

TABLE OF CONTENTS

Introduction 8

What kind of person is typically charged with DUI and how intoxicated are they on average? 9

But what are the typical circumstances that lead people to be arrested in the first place? 15

...Is there a clear legal definition of what drunk driving actually is? 17

Is there a Common Blood Alcohol Level You See? What's the Highest BAC You've Ever Seen? 20

How Common is it to be Charged for DUI Due to Drugs vs. Alcohol? 24

How Does Medical Marijuana Affect DUI Charges and Convictions? 27

Is There a Common Scenario Where Doing 'X' Will Either Get You Arrested or Get You Out of Trouble? 30

Is There a Particular Story You Hear Over and Over? .. 34

How Have You Seen People Typically React To A DUI Arrest? 37

What Advice Do You have for Someone Who Has Just Been Pulled Over? 43

What is The Best Way to Refuse a Field Sobriety Test? 46

Are There Situations Where Taking a Blood Test Is a Good Idea? 47

What percentage of DUI cases go to trial? 49

Is It Better To Go To Trial, Plead, or Settle a DUI Case? 52

Can a DUI Conviction Be Expunged? (removed, sealed, or deleted from your record) 54

What Aspects of a DUI Do People Have The Most Emotional Difficulties Dealing With? 55

Are Current DUI Laws Too Harsh? 58

How Much Does A DUI Cost? 68

What Are the Advantages of Hiring a DUI Attorney? .. 72

How Do You Get Suitable Legal Representation to Defend Your DUI? 80

Why Do You Practice DUI Law? 82

What's The Most Important Thing You Want to Say to People Charged With a DUI Who Read This Book? 86

Introduction

Movie stars and sports stars are arrested and accused of drunk driving literally every single day. Maybe you've driven through DUI checkpoints in your state. It's highly likely a friend, family member, or someone you know has been arrested for DUI / DWI.

Currently, the approximate number of Americans arrested for driving under the influence is between 1 and 2 million people a year. That's a TON of people – about 37 football stadiums' worth!

I was curious as to the truth behind what really goes on, who gets arrested and why, and how the process works. Over the past 18 months, I ended up interviewing over 26 DUI lawyers from across the county about their experiences in defending clients.

Some of their answers were entertaining, some frightening, and most were extremely eye-opening. Drunk driving is not at all what it seems. What follows is a compilation of answers from these attorneys to questions such as:

Are Drunk Drivers really 'drunk' or just DUI (driving under the influence)?

Are you truly intoxicated at the "legal limit" of 0.08 blood alcohol level (BAC)?

Do only bad people get arrested for DUI?

When is the Most Common Time and Where's the Most Common Place to be Pulled Over and Arrested on Suspicion of DUI?

Note on the Use of Terms:

Depending on the state you live in, this offense can be called: DUI (driving under the influence), DWI (driving while intoxicated), OWI (operating while intoxicated), OVI (operating a vehicle while intoxicated), DWAI (driving while ability impaired), Drunk Driving, etc.

Let's get started finding out the real truth of what goes on out there…

WHAT KIND OF PERSON IS TYPICALLY CHARGED WITH DUI AND HOW INTOXICATED ARE THEY ON AVERAGE?

Are more men vs. women charged with DUI? Older or younger people? Rich or poor?

Demographically, because we're Reno, Nevada we get a lot of visitors to our area. I would say a few more men than women although I would say that the women are a little bit more discriminated against because of the manner and method in which the breath machines work. 60% of them are first-timers where the typical situation is that they had an extra glass of wine for dinner and they just don't realize how close that .08 limit can be.

(Attorney Ken Stover - Reno, Nevada)

... in my practice I've found that there really isn't any particular set of circumstances or factors or demographics that DUIs apply to. They apply to men, they apply to women, they apply to people who are under 21, people who are in their early 20s, people who are much older, different racial backgrounds, first time offenders, multiple offenses, I see quite a few different things and I don't think that statistically speaking there is one demographic that shows a  stronger trend toward receiving a DUI than any other particular demographic. And that's kind of what I find fascinating about it. It seems to be one of the few criminal offenses that affects people of all walks of life, all socio-economic, racial, age backgrounds, all those things.

(Attorney Zach Westerfield - Denver, Colorado)

You know, I've found that both people and clients are across the board. I've seen people that are under the limit charged, I've seen people that should be legally dead charged, I've represented lawyers and doctors charged with DUI, I've seen hardworking blue-collar people charged with DUI.

(Attorney Michael Byrne - Chicago, Illinois)

I would say between men and women, it's about a 50/50 split; many times, there are people that are involved in bad circumstances like there's been a death in the family or they're going through a nasty divorce, something traumatic has happened in their lives that made them change their normal routine pattern that involves more drinking and they make a mistake in judgment and end up in a bad situation.
(Attorney Dale Naticchia - Cleveland, Ohio)

Well first of all, DUI is an equal opportunity employer that happens to all people across all ages, and across all socio-economic classes. So I would say there's no stereotypical DUI, it's actually the kind of thing that can happen to anyone. There are two typical DUI defendant circumstances, however.

There's the one person who really is an alcoholic and has a problem with alcohol, and either has multiple DUIs because of it, or simply has a problem because they are always drinking they are likely to get a DUI whenever they are stopped.

The other is the regular, ordinary person, who is not an alcoholic, generally a good and responsible person, but on one particular incident uses bad judgment and/or got unlucky on one particular day, and ended up being accused of DUI as a result." he continues to add: *"I would say that the percentage of alcoholics is fairly small, I haven't done any statistical analysis, but less than 20%. 80% of the people are like I said, in the category of using bad judgment on one particular day and happened to get unlucky.*
(Attorney Anthony Lowenstein - San Francisco, California)

I would say that the majority of the clients I represent are normally first time offenders. I do have a number of repeat clients that come back that have been arrested for a new DUI, but the vast majority - over 99% - of my clients are first-time offenders. They tend to be overwhelmingly male, but there is a fairly high percentage of females. In terms of circumstance, they really come from all walks of life.

(Attorney Brendan Kelly - Omaha, Nebraska)

Well the one thing about DUI case is that I have found that it pretty much breaks out evenly across the spectrum but it seems to be for the most part the ones who seem to get in the most trouble seem to be younger individuals who are just learning about drinking and driving . They are coming out of college and they are used to probably walking across campus to go out for their drinks and now they get in their cars. You can't do that. If you have anything in your system they'll hammer you with a DUI. And traditionally I would say 50% of the people I represent tend to be first time offenders.

(Attorney Marc Taiani - Pittsburgh, Pennsylvania)

You're going to find what I would say are people that are just like you and me, they are fine, upstanding individuals that are professional and they are not out there to do something wrong, they are not out there to do something that is illegal, that's not what their intent was at the start of the day. They got caught doing something that maybe they shouldn't have been doing, but that doesn't mean that they are a bad person. In terms of the standard client, beyond a lot of them being first-time DUI defendants, there's really no defining characteristic, it's not that you are going to find lots of men, or lots of women, lots of eighteen year olds or forty-five year olds.

I've had everything from kids fresh out of high school, that are not twenty-one yet, and they have other issues because they are not twenty-one, to people that are like you and me that are professionals, to airplane pilots that if they get a DUI then they're going to lose their ability to work because they lose their license. I have had military DUIs that are also looking at non-judicial punishment (NJP). There's as many different DUI clients as there is anything else in the world.

(Attorney Joshua Hale - San Diego, California)

You know, it's really interesting; there certainly are characteristics of an individual common to people arrested for drunk driving. But it really cuts across all barriers, all lines, all types of individuals. Certainly, there are more first-time offenders and I think that that's fortunate for the fact that that shows that at least people are getting the message and I think the message is obviously so severe in California and Los Angeles for the first time that it does cut down the recidivism of people arrested for subsequent offenses. Certainly, more men are arrested than women and probably the age groups tends to be more between twenty-five and forty-five for the majority of individuals arrested for drunk driving.

(Attorney Lawrence Wolf - Los Angeles, California)

The way it breaks down is about 50% of the people are first-timers. They've been arrested for a DUI First. In most cases they've never ever had another criminal case, they've never been arrested for anything else and they just kind of slipped up and got arrested. ... The other 50% are people with DUI Second, Third or Fourth offenses, and they've really done this over a long period of time and it kind of coincides with times that they've been depressed or times that they were having a good time and were out drinking and partying and ended up having a DUI. But most first time offenders do not become repeat offenders. In terms of demographics, age I would say between 20 and 30, more men than women, probably 60% men 40% women.

(Attorney Fred Woods - Greenville, South Carolina)

...it's amazing to me how there really is no, typical, prototypical defendant in a traffic DUI case, so you're going to see a lot of people who have never been in trouble in their lives who are grandmothers, parents, professionals, executives, lawyers, stockbrokers, marketers, I mean, every level of person could go out, have a night out with friends or with family or a work function, and come home, have too much to drink and suddenly they're looking for an attorney.

(Attorney Doug Riddell - Columbus, Ohio)

So far, it seems like pretty much all walks of life, all ages, and types of folks get arrested for DUI...

BUT WHAT ARE THE TYPICAL CIRCUMSTANCES THAT LEAD PEOPLE TO BE ARRESTED IN THE FIRST PLACE?

DUIs tend to have a very predictable series of events. Now these are DUIs that don't involve collisions.

They all invariably involve an officer who has a problem about the way someone's driving. They may be going too fast, which indicates impairment, or they may be going too slow, and they'll say that indicates impairment. Their lights may be on in an area that's well lit, and they'll say that alcohol has affected their vision and they'll have a problem with that.

They may not like the way the car stopped, maybe they stopped too far past the stop bar, maybe they stopped too soon, maybe they're moving too much inside their lane, maybe outside their lane. There's going to be a complaint about the driving. Police officer activates their lights and the driver is pulled over.

Police officer's usually going to have a problem with the way the person's pulled over, pulled over too soon, pulled over too late, didn't like where they pulled over, didn't like the way they pulled over. There'll be something in the report that says the way they pulled over indicates possible impairment.

They're going to ask for license and registration, they're going to report that the person appeared to be confused and slow in his motions and when they finally gave them the license and registration they also gave them a coffee card.

(Attorney Steve Tinsley - Orlando, Florida)

There may not be a specific type of person that is charged with DUI, DWI or OVI, even though there may be a common chain of events that leads to being charged. It makes you wonder, what IS drunk driving? Why are there so many terms to describe it?

...IS THERE A CLEAR LEGAL DEFINITION OF WHAT DRUNK DRIVING ACTUALLY IS?

Well, the way that it works in Colorado is that you can be charged with a DWAI which is known as 'Driving While Ability Impaired' if you have a BAC that's actually registered by a breath test or a blood test of .05 to .09. And I've only had a few cases where someone has come to me and their BAC was in the DWAI range, the vast majority of cases people  have a BAC that is greater than .08, which puts them in the DUI or Driving Under the Influence category, the more serious of the two charges.

I have a few cases where people are in the higher range in Colorado, where it's mandatory jail time even for a first offense, when you have a BAC that is higher than .20...
        (Attorney Zach Westerfield - Denver, Colorado)

It's a good inquiry, as a lot of people even present that to me "I wasn't drunk. How did I get a DWI or s DUI?" That's because it's a scientific test not based on whether or not you feel drunk and that's where the subtlety comes in. But however, the police are responsible for performing field sobriety tests, which do give them indicators or marks for regular people whether or not they can walk a straight line or do the

alphabet correctly and do things that full drunk person would have difficulty with or for someone who is impaired by alcohol.
(Attorney Carl Spector - Fair Lawn, New Jersey)

Well in Nebraska we actually have two separate standards. We have the .08 is the legal limit, so anything above that would be considered under the influence. A 0.15 is considered an aggravated DUI. The majority of my clients fall closer to the aggravated range,

I would say roughly 15% of my clients may have a blood alcohol closer to .08, somewhere between the 0.08 and .15 range, and around 35% fall over the 0.15 aggravated range which requires a mandatory jail sentence. The other would fall somewhere between .08 and 0.15.
(Attorney Brendan Kelly - Omaha, Nebraska)

.08 is the legal level. If you're above .08, you're driving under the influence, it doesn't matter whether you are inebriated or not. With that being said, .08 depending on the person's size, someone with my size, I'm around 200 lbs, .08 could be one and half beers or one strong beer in under an hour, if you are a 200lb guy one beer in an hour may not do a whole lot to you in terms of level of inebriation, and that's going on just the general feeling "boy, I don't feel drunk".

Also, there's experts that say, one beer may not as impair someone as much as we previously thought.

That doesn't mean that they're not legally under the influence, but there's a difference between being legally under the *influence and the second charge to driving actually under the influence.*

There's two charges when you are charged with DUI, an "A" and a "B" count, one is the .08 that everyone knows, the other is driving under the influence, some people may not be under the influence at .08, and some people may be under the influence at .04. It's really a very personal thing, and because of that they went to a .08 number but I don't know that that number is necessarily fair for all circumstances.

(Attorney Joshua Hale - San Diego, California)

Well, there's essentially two ways you can be charged with DUI alcohol. One is DUI per se where you have over a 0.08 Blood Alcohol Content and the other way is DUI less safe and that one doesn't require any evidence of what your Blood Alcohol Content is, but it requires that the state prove that you're not in control of the motor vehicle and that you're under the influence of alcohol to the extent you were less safe to drive. So if you do do a breath test and you blow under a 0.08, the state is forced to try and prove the case as a less safe to drive case you know, similar to if you refuse the test, that's the statute that they're trying to prosecute you under...

Now, I think the state has a lot of trouble proving cases where the person's Blood Alcohol Content is under 0.08. I think a lot of people, you will ask a random person on the street, they would think that if they took the breath test under a 0.08 then they're not going to be arrested for DUI....A lot of juries are not going to convict when they hear that the person took the breath test as requested and their Blood Alcohol Content was under the 0.08 'legal limit'.

(Attorney Kavan Grover - Atlanta, Georgia)

Ok, so there's "Drunk Driving", "Legally Impaired", "Ability Impaired", "Intoxicated", "Above .08", and more terms, but what it seems to boil down to is that DUI involves 2 different charges:

The concentration of alcohol in your blood, breath or urine exceeds a certain level (per se charge)

You show evidence that you're literally, physically impaired (i.e. you're drunk, your speech is slurred, you have bad balance, or other physical, verbal or behavioral indicators) and operating, driving, sitting in, sleeping in, or around a 'vehicle'. Confused yet as to what it means to be driving under the influence?

IS THERE A COMMON BLOOD ALCOHOL LEVEL YOU SEE? WHAT'S THE HIGHEST BAC YOU'VE EVER SEEN?

I would probably surprise you to tell you that I prosecuted a .54. To give you an idea, a .30 is toxicologically comatose, although people can get above a .30 if they have a lot of practice. .40 is toxicologically dead, so I prosecuted someone who was at a .54, and I defended a young lady who was at a .62, and you wouldn't be surprised to know that she was in a

coma for three weeks before she could even be released from the hospital after that event. But those are very rare. You see things that are triple the legal limit, that happens, and I would say 20% of my cases are above the .18 level.
(Attorney Ken Stover - Reno, Nevada)

A lot that are probably a little bit below the limit and some that will go up to a .13. Obviously there are those that are higher and in New York State we have .18 is an aggravated driving while intoxicated. But because the atmosphere on Long Island, and the police officers are pulling people over for anything that they think can be a DWI a lot of people are coming in now with a low reading.
(Attorney Eric Sachs - Bellmore, New York)

You know, I've found that both people and clients are across the board. I've seen people that are under the limit charged, I've seen people that should be legally dead charged.
(Attorney Michael Byrne - Chicago, Illinois)

I think, probably the highest limit I ever had was a client who not only had a 0.40 (and the limit being 0.08) but he also had LSD in his system. I think that was an extreme situation. Certainly, for first time offenders there's a much wider range, I think you'll see individuals on first time offense is certainly close to the 0.08 limit and also going up to the 0.20 limit.
(Attorney Lawrence Wolf - Los Angeles, California)

Oh, gosh, I mean I've had the range from a .28 just came in the door actually a couple to a .002, a guy pulled over and literally had had maybe some mouthwash but had some leg injuries and got pulled over for a traffic stop, and suddenly getting charged with an OVI. So it really does range all over the spectrum with me

(Attorney Doug Riddell - Columbus, Ohio)

I'll tell you one story, and it's about a guy and it's really astonishing to think that something like this could ever happen. I had a guy whose wife actually worked for the Indiana Supreme Court, and he came to my office for a DUI and I was supposed to meet him here at 9 o'clock, I got to my office a few minutes before that, there was a truck parked out in my parking lot, but nobody was in there.

So I waited until about 9:15, walked out to the truck and saw somebody in the truck sleeping. And I kind of knocked on the door and got no response. And then I banged on the window and still didn't get anything, and I thought: Gee, Jesus this guy is dead. ….. And in between his legs was an open beer can and a drip from his mouth was some spittle.

And so I finally roused this guy and he got up and came into my office. In my briefcase I have a portable breath machine that I've used a hundred times and I gave it to my client. My client tested .41 in my office. For most people, .20 would be falling down drunk and ungodly sick. .30, if you can even get there, in most cases is toxic.

And my guy was driving at .40. So I called his wife, and I said: Look, I've been doing this for a long time and I've never had anyone arrested at my office but your husband is not leaving my office. So she came and got him, took him to the hospital and we ended up working out that case to nobody's surprise.

He was just a horrific alcoholic, but again, I've had brain surgeons that have operated on people at .15 and so if you are a chronic alcoholic, you can be as they call it, walking drunk, and appear perfectly fine.

(Attorney Steve Litz - Monrovia, Indiana)

Don't forget that it's not just alcohol that can lead to a DUI charge. In some states, driving under the influence of drugs, both prescription or illegal, can lead to a drug-based DUI charge.

Yes, there have been many charges of DUI for taking Xanax, Anti-depressants, other prescription drugs, and illegal drugs such as Marijuana, Cocaine, Ecstasy and more.

HOW COMMON IS IT TO BE CHARGED FOR DUI DUE TO DRUGS VS. ALCOHOL?

[I am seeing] mostly alcohol but there's either some combo cases where you're going to see alcohol and drugs. And there's in Ohio especially now there's a lot of these prescription drug issues, that we have going on. And I actually see a lot of those kind of cases now where you see someone who is clearly impaired but they don't know what it is. And actually those can be in many ways more difficult for the state or the government to prove against someone because they don't know what it is.

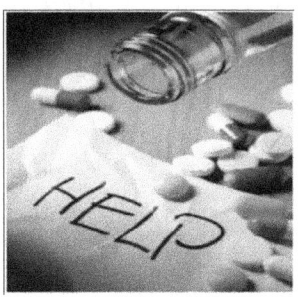

And if they don't take a urine test or even if they do, the evidence that you're going to be able to introduce, a urine test into the court system is much more complicated than the breath machines that they use. So in many ways, if you get a drug charge for a DUI, it's going to be an easier case to beat.

(Attorney Doug Riddell - Columbus, Ohio)

There are a far greater number of individuals who are arrested for driving under the influence of alcohol versus driving under the influence of drugs and the reason therefore, I think is twofold. One is that individuals consume more alcohol than they do drugs and there's a greater amount of individuals who obviously consume alcohol and then drive.....Also, I think that the effect of drugs is not always the same as the effect of alcohol on individuals and in fact, therefore, the amount of alcohol a person may consume would cause their driving to be greater impaired than if they had consumed some type of drug.

(Attorney Lawrence Wolf - Los Angeles, California)

I think that that in administrative cases, you are seeing a combination, but with the state criminal charges they are filing for alcohol, or a combination of alcohol and a controlled substance – drug under the influence charges. And there's never a different reason for that. Prescription drug use often are controlled substances, sometimes they are not, but the state likes to use the additive effects …..

[The additive effect is] basically, if you use a prescription drug, and that prescription drug is a controlled substance, and let's say you had very little alcohol use, or you had half of a beverage or one beverage and you take a breath test and you are not even blowing over that legal limit – if the prosecution can prove that the prescription drug use in combination with the alcohol enhanced the effects of the alcohol, then you can be found guilty of a DUI here in Oregon.

(Attorney Shannon Wilson - Portland, Oregon)

I'd say that in recent years we're seeing more and more drug DUI. And one thing that people are generally unaware of but need to keep in mind is that you can get a DUI while under the influence of prescription medication, and not even an illegal drug. But if a drug impairs your ability to drive, you can be charged with DUI.

(Attorney Michael Byrne - Chicago, Illinois)

[I am seeing] mostly alcohol, although it's not uncommon to get a case where, in fact, when the person is arrested, they do a search of the car and they come up with paraphernalia or marijuana.

Testing for drugs there are, in Ohio, there are levels for certain drugs in your system including marijuana....and it's becoming more common that I see prescription drugs, that's mostly what I see and even though you are taking the drug as prescribed by the pharmacist, if you are under the influence or impaired and the officer can say 'he was acting sleepy, it didn't seem like he knew what he was doing', you'll be charged with an OVI and I've had many cases where people were taking drugs such as Soma or Xanax in the prescribed dosage and they ended up being charged.

     (Attorney Dale Naticchia - Cleveland, Ohio)

I think the vast majority of the cases are alcohol cases. I think studies have been done and a lot of people that are DUI are actually under the influence of other things as well whether it be marijuana or cocaine or something else but the reality of it is, there's not that many people that take drugs and don't consume any alcohol and for the most part,

if you're out on the road and you have alcohol, any amount of alcohol in you, the officer is going to just suspect DUI alcohol and have a hard time detecting the presence of any other drug.

I would say that probably only about ten to fifteen percent of the cases I've seen are DUI drug cases. Most of them are alcohol cases. …… I think that even when the officers do *suspect that there's a possibility of drugs and alcohol, a lot of them will just pursue the alcohol side of it because they don't want to have to go through the hassle of taking a person to the hospital to get their blood taken.*

(Attorney Kavan Grover - Atlanta, Georgia)

In the last 10 years, Medical Marijuana has become a huge topic. In 16 of the United States, medical marijuana use is now approved and patients are legally able (under state law) to buy and use marijuana if they have a valid medical prescription. Marijuana use, possession, distribution, etc is still ILLEGAL under Federal Law, however. But how does this play into DUI?

How Does Medical Marijuana Affect DUI Charges and Convictions?

[To be guilty of] Marijuana [intoxication] it's ten out of grams to one milliliter of urine (sic.), they have to do a urine or blood test, that's a very low level and in marijuana, the marijuana metabolites stay in your system for approximately twenty-eight days so it could have a cumulative effect and you might not have smoked for two days, they stop and believe you are impaired, do a urine analysis and find out that you are over the legal limit for marijuana.

(Attorney Dale Naticchia - Cleveland, Ohio)

Editor Note: Ohio does not currently have medical marijuana laws.

The Georgia Appellate Courts have said, they've made a ruling in the late 1990s that some judges only apply to marijuana but it was recently clarified and it says that if you are under the influence of any drug that could possibly be legally prescribed or legally used then the state absolutely has to show that your intoxication under that, based on that drug has to have made you less safe to drive for you to be guilty of DUI drugs and for any case that falls under that purview, whether it be a marijuana case or a morphine case or most classes of amphetamines, it can be difficult for the state to prove that that drug actually rendered you less safe to drive.....

I think there's a lot of cases [where the defendant hasn't used drugs in a while] especially with marijuana since it stays in your system for a long time. A lot of people, if they do get blood tested, they're going to show a small amount of marijuana and absence of other evidence that's not just going to be enough for the state to prove a DUI case.

(Attorney Kavan Grover - Atlanta, Georgia)

Editor Note: Georgia does not currently have medical marijuana laws.

Well if you're asked to give a blood or urine test you will have been arrested at that point, the officer will have had to establish probable cause that you are under the influence, in this case marijuana before they can take you in and have you provide that sample.

So whether you are going to be charged for DUI I would say yes initially, but they might write you a citation for DUI, and bring in an expert that says, yes your behavior demonstrates that of someone who uses marijuana and that you were slow driving or fast driving, or something that driving under the influence of marijuana would produce.

But it doesn't really change whether you were using medical marijuana or marijuana. The key here is that based on the observations and based on the results of the test – can they prove that at the time of driving you were impaired. So that's the key here.

(Attorney Shannon Wilson - Portland, Oregon)

Editor Note: Oregon DOES have medical marijuana laws in place.

When the police lights go on behind you and you've had a few drinks, what to do next may be a mystery. Although all DUI arrests can be prevented by not driving if you've had ANYTHING to drink, smoke, injest, inject or snort, in situations where it's "too late", what you do after the police have stopped you can determine whether you'll make it home or get arrested

So what do you do if you're out there, driving around and you've had one or more drinks and the red and blue flash behind you?

Is there a common set of circumstances where most people tend to get pulled over and arrested?

How about some "secrets" to avoiding getting pulled over or "getting out of" a DUI arrest?

IS THERE A COMMON SCENARIO WHERE DOING 'X' WILL EITHER GET YOU ARRESTED OR GET YOU OUT OF TROUBLE?

Although every story is unique, there are some common DUI scenarios that are acted out, over and over. Here are some attorneys' stories about WHY their clients ended up....being their clients. They also share some of the behaviors that caused them to be pulled over.

Well one thing I find frequently is that people who are charged with DUI are many times within a mile of their home, so whether it's they are just running out to get something at the store, they didn't think that just driving a mile is a problem, or whether it's they are almost home and they make a mistake, they let their defenses down, for whatever reason there's a very high frequency of people who are charged with DUI when they are close to their home at the time.

(Attorney Michael - Byrne Chicago, Illinois)

.... most of them involve someone's gone out, whether to a friend's house or to a party or to a restaurant or to a bar and they've had a few drinks and they're driving home. ... Now, there are all sorts of cases, I mean, you get people that are completely intoxicated in the middle of the day, you get some

people that go to sleep after a night of heavy drinking and get pulled over in the morning and they still have a pretty high Blood Alcohol Content.

(Attorney Kavan Grover - Atlanta, Georgia)

Typically the client that comes in the door is going to be coming from a bar. That's typically going to be the circumstances, especially here in Ohio where you're talking about an area that's more spread out than if you are living in an area like Chicago or New York City or something like that.

If you're out at a bar, you might be 10, 15 miles from home, so that leads to having a few too many drinks and then just trying – in this area, calling a cab is the way to go obviously, but it's not always easy at 1 in the morning in Columbus, OH, or anywhere in Ohio for that matter.

(Attorney Doug Riddell - Columbus, Ohio)

I had a client who was out with a couple of friends of his, and the friends were boyfriend/girlfriend. And he was just out, he was a drinker, and one of them was the driver. The boyfriend/girlfriend got into a fight, and she wanted my client to take her home. He was just being a good friend. Well, he lost his job, a very good job. He had a special license.

He had a license that was class A license so he couldn't drive for his company anymore. That just – it can happen to anyone anytime. I've got another client that just picked up a second DUI.

He didn't learn his lesson the first time unfortunately. He kept drinking, and he wasn't intending to drive.

But for some reason, instead of getting a ride or walking like he intended to do, he was so drunk that he just grabbed his keys and went. Another client just recently here in San Francisco was just looking to move their car.

They walked to where they drank, they walked home. And there were so drunk that they thought got to move the car, can't get a ticket, can't get it towed. Accident, hit and run, DUI.

(Attorney Aaron Bortel - San Francisco, California)

I get a lot of cases where police officers say well I pulled them over because their tail light was out or their license plate light was not on. Or something extraordinarily minor. It is not usually the case where they say oh he's weaving all over the road. These are what I would call probably practice pullovers where they just kind of pull them over and the police officer's intent is to give them a warning.

They get up to the person and they smell alcohol on the breath and that's what sets up the full investigation. It is perfectly acceptable under Michigan law to pullover someone for a civil infraction,

a common traffic ticket such as defective equipment where a tail light may be out, didn't use a turn signal, or like I said a license plate light might be out. But this is where the vast majority of drunk driving cases I've seen come from.

…. It's usually these what seems to be innocuous situations that turn into something more.

(Attorney Stuart Collis - Ypsilanti, Michigan)

...A lot of times people come home with a designated driver and then go back out to the store to get milk, or cigarettes and it's I'm only driving 2 blocks or around the corner and that is when they have the encounter with the police.... I have had people that crashed into the tree next door. I have had people who have come home, gone back out to the store and then were waiting at the traffic light on their way home and then somebody else rear ended them.

That's how the police came to the scene and then they were arrested for the driving while intoxicated. SO unlike other crimes where people actually go in and they steal something or they actually commit a crime, some of the circumstances of DWI's are just unavoidable.

You could be as careful as possible but there are still other people on the road. And there are still obstacles and we hear a lot of that. People get in court that way.

(Attorney Eric Sachs - Bellmore, New York)

What they [Police] really do is arrest as many people as they can for things as small as improper lane change, or they looked like something was going on, and they see if they can make a case on them. A lot of times they'll get people right down the street from a popular bar and they'll have a checkpoint to see if people are drinking or they're driving.

(Attorney Fred Woods - Greenville, South Carolina)

Even though there's a thousand little things that may get you pulled over, the excuses that people tell the police are surprisingly similar...

Is There a Particular Story You Hear Over and Over?

A lot of people simply say "I only had a few drinks and it was many many hours before I started driving - how could I be responsible of charge of DWI?" and that is a theme.
　　　　　(Attorney Carl Spector - Fair Lawn, New Jersey)

Well, yes, I mean, it's pretty standard that you hear, "two or three drinks"
　　　　　(Attorney Kavan Grover - Atlanta, Georgia)

Yes the proverbial 'two beers'. You never want to tell the police officer that you had two beers. You know, from wherever it started - from the beginning of driving under the influence to today's time, the joke is, is that the person 'only had two beers'. So I will say that's probably the most common situation.

      (Attorney Lawrence Wolf - Los Angeles, California)

Well it's always the same, and the police know it too, it's: Well I only had three beers tonight.

      (Attorney Steve Tinsley - Orlando, Florida)

I think for a typical first time offender, the story I hear over and over is in essence boils down to "I had one or two drinks too many, and the end result was my usual good judgment left me, and I got behind the wheel thinking I was fine to drive." And I find that it typically appears to be true.

      (Attorney John English - Lansing, Michigan)

I hear, there's no way that my blood alcohol level could be that high. I hear that constantly from people. You know, people will tell the police they had nothing to drink, one drinks, two drinks is the most popular answer.

But no, it happens a lot, and very often they didn't have as much to drink as the number, and that can be because they're still absorbing alcohol but also what people don't realize is the way that these drinks are measured. Most beer is close to if not over now 5%. Almost all the micro-beers, and some are 7, 8, 9%.

A glass of wine is measured at 4 or 5 ounces. If you look at the size of a wine glass, some of these glasses are 16 to 18 ounces, and you want someone who gives you a pour, they don't want to make it seem like a small pour, so they'll give you 7 or 8 ounces or sometimes more in a glass of wine, and that's what people pour for themselves.

And the alcohol content has gone up so much in recent years, so if you've got a 7 or 8 ounce glass of fine that's 14 or 15% alcohol, that's going to be like 2 potentially 2 plus drinks, and if you had two of those and you don't weigh very much, you acan be way over the limit because that can be like 4 or 5 drinks.And you know if you haven't anything to eat, it absorbs pretty quickly, then you're looking at being well over the limit if it's all recent drinking before the drive. So I think that I didn't have that much to drink is the most popular, the most common thread or statement that I hear from clients.

(Attorney Aaron Bortel - San Francisco, California)

The majority of the people say 'I wasn't doing anything wrong'. The police officer pulled me over and he said that my speech was slurred.

He said that I was speeding. He said all the traffic things. I hear the same thing over and again. I only had one drink. I only had two drinks. What people have to understand is that we live in a society now where people don't want us to drink and drive at all.

(Attorney Eric Sachs - Bellmore, New York)

Well I mean everyone, the most important thing that I hear from I think every single person that comes in here is I didn't think I was that intoxicated. And the bottom line is, if you have anything, anything at all in your system you can be pulled over.

(Attorney Marc Taiani - Pittsburgh, Pennsylvania)

Hopefully, dear reader, you never experience this, but for morbid curiosity's sake, what does it FEEL LIKE to be arrested for drunk driving and go through the criminal process?

How Have You Seen People Typically React To A DUI Arrest?

Well generally the number one emotion I see is that people are scared. They are scared that they're going to lose their driver's license and their ability to pick up their kids from school, go get groceries, go get medicines, and it also affects your ability to get to work and put food on the table for your family. But then there's also fear about the criminal side as well, people are scared about going to jail – that's a number one concern.

(Attorney Justin Summary - St Louis, Missouri)

Well, that's kind of an interesting question because the first time offenders, especially the ones who are good hard working individuals who just had a bit too much to drink on one given day celebrating a party or wedding are just highly embarrassed. They are just trying to protect their loved ones.

They don't even want their loved ones to know about the situation and they want to make sure everything is kept confidential which of course it is.

With the people who have had subsequent offenses they are more resigned as to the process. They know what is going on, they've been through it before. They are more concerned about mitigating their own damages. What I've also found with people who have a serious problem, those who are unwilling to admit they have a problem, they will always say they only had two drinks that night.

(Attorney Stuart Collis - Ypsilanti, Michigan)

Well I think the most people they take responsibility for their actions. Most people are embarrassed. They are embarrassed more than anything else by a DUI. But what they don't realize is how much this affects their life. Specifically if you are looking for a job down the road and your future employer do a criminal background check these things pop up. Not only is it embarrassing but it can keep you from getting a job. The next issue that people don't realize is the licenses suspension attached.

If you are not eligible for a first time offender program, you are looking at a minimum of 12-18 months license suspension. And if you work, as most people in this country and state do you don't walk to work.

You have to drive. And if you lose your licenses there's no way you are going to be able to get to work.... You are going to lose your job. So even though people are apologetic they want to *they don't think out the consequences before they act. And I think most people are just trying to do the right thing.*

(Attorney Marc Taiani - Pittsburgh, Pennsylvania)

You know probably the biggest insight is the fact that for some reason, people think they can talk themselves out of it. They think that if they explain it enough, say the right things, act in a certain way, that they will not end up getting arrested...The reality is that almost all the time, if in fact you've been drinking and you have alcohol on your breath, you're going to be arrested. So that attempt to try to talk your way out of it, that attempt to try to explain it, is really only going to provide additional evidence for the prosecutor. So probably the best advice is to be polite but say as little as possible.

(Attorney Lawrence Wolf - Los Angeles, California)

….it's very sad and very frustrating for them, because they trust these police people, whether it's somebody who's been on the force for a year, or someone who's been on the force for 20 years, they expect those people to be above reproach. And the truth is that in many of these cases, something is in the police report that just plain did not happen, and for that reason 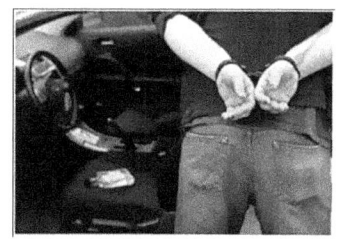 *it's tough because my client is now being called a criminal, the police report is made by a police person for all intents is the person who the court tends to believe, whether that's the judge or whether that goes to jury. One of the things I've heard at jury level is "Well, they wouldn't be going to trial if they*

weren't guilty" and that's just not true. In terms of the actual clients, there's a lot of anger, a lot of frustration, and that goes to those that are just plain guilty, or those that should probably not be charged with a DUI.

It's very frustrating for those clients that probably should be charged with a DUI because I can't just make the case disappear...
                    (Attorney Joshua Hale - San Diego, California)

Well first of all, it starts from the very beginning, being stopped by a policeman. They ask you to do a field sobriety test, people are scared out of their wits, they don't know what to think, they're not listening, all they're thinking is they're in trouble and the officer.... People are embarrassed, people don't know what's going to happen to them, they don't know how it's going to affect their lives, they don't know how they're going to get through it..
                    (Attorney Dale Naticchia - Cleveland, Ohio)

Well, I think, first of all, most people, if they haven't received advice from a DUI attorney in the past; they cooperate with everything the law enforcement asks them to do. They do all the field sobriety tests, they do the breath tests, they, a lot of people think that they're going to be able to talk their way out of the DUI charge and most of them are unsuccessful.

I think, most people think that they can tell the officer they've had one or two drinks and that's the end and the officer is going to take them for their word and stop their investigation but everyone, everyone reacts differently to being stopped by *the officers, I mean, you certainly get some cases where people refuse to say anything to the law enforcement officer, so there's a wide variety of reactions that people have.*

(Attorney Kavan Grover - Atlanta, Georgia)

Well probably the number one thing, when they're arrested for the first time, they're scared. Most people are scared when blue lights go on behind them when they're driving, they're scared when they get pulled out of the vehicle and have to do these field sobriety tests, they're very nervous, then they get put in jail for the first time ever, spending the night in jail, they come out of it worried about the consequences it's going to have on the rest of their lives. So that's the number one thing is people are truly scared.

The second thing that I would say is that most people believe that they are not purposefully committing a crime.

They feel that they've waited long enough and that they're OK. And there are two reasons, and this is probably going beyond your question but there are two reasons why people – responsible people – would end up with a DUI. 1) They don't realize how slowly alcohol eliminates from their system. They think that by waiting a couple of hours they'll be OK and that's simply not true. 2) There's a thing called the Mellanby Effect – once you start drinking alcohol, you start feeling the effects of the alcohol on your way up, once you're on your way down, you don't feel the effects of the alcohol – so you could be at a .08 and be feeling kind of intoxicated on the way up, on the way down you may be at a .08/.10 and you feel completely fine. So if you get pulled over for speeding, tail light out, you drop your cell phone, you cross the line, the next thing you know you're arrested, you take a breath test and you're convicted of a DUI.

(Attorney Michael Tillotson - Virginia Beach, Virginia)

Again 90% of my cases are first-time DUIs and it normally does not rub people the right way when they realize that for the first time in their life they've been criminalized, and have been treated like criminals.

They've had the police stop them, detain them, handcuff them. It really is a slap in anyone's face to an otherwise law-abiding citizen, who suddenly has become a criminal. So people have a certain amount of indignation, and for the first time they are being threatened with having a criminal record, having their rights violated, their license suspended, so people have a lot of strong reactions at first. At the same time, I have seen a lot of people be contrite and have a lot of self-awareness and acknowledge that they need to take responsibility, have made a mistake and want to pay the consequences, but also want to move on with their life as quickly as possible.

(Attorney Anthony Lowenstein - San Francisco, California)

Well what I've learned from representing thousands of clients is that people like to talk. People rarely exercise their right to remain silent, they just talk and talk and it's important to realize that every question that the police ask you has a purpose. The purpose is to convict you later in court. They are not asking you these questions because they are bored, or for fun.

When they ask you "Where are you coming from," "What did you drink", "What time did you last eat or sleep?" Each of these questions has a purpose. I have police officers that get arrested for DUI and they talk, so it amazes me how people cannot resist the urge to just volunteer all sorts of information, a lot of which is incriminating. ... A great case could easily turn into a horrible case as they talk more and more and volunteer more information.

(Attorney Jeff Yeh - Los Angeles, California)

Of course, it's unethical and against the law to give advice to people how to avoid being arrested for DUI if they have been drinking or using certain drugs, but there ARE things you can do to not make your situation worse.

WHAT ADVICE DO YOU HAVE FOR SOMEONE WHO HAS JUST BEEN PULLED OVER?

Well the thing I tell most people is that they are not required to give the officer much information. If they ask you, "where are you going" or what not, you are not obligated to tell them. The thing I tell people is to keep their insurance, license and registration in a set place, where it's easy to get to and have it prepared to give the officer when you get stopped because that's what they are going to ask for. The second thing to remember is that the roadside tests are voluntary. What the officer is trying to do is isolate you so he can determine whether or not the odor of alcohol is on your person or in your vehicle. So I would recommend to everyone that if the officer asks them to step outside of the car, they inquire why they have to step outside of the car.

(Attorney Brendan Kelly - Omaha, Nebraska)

Well I'd say that before you even get in the car you need to make sure that you have your driver's license on you, that you have your registration and proof of insurance, and keep that someplace easily accessible to you. That way the officer isn't waiting at the window while you are fumbling around trying to find these documents and then giving the officer the opportunity to stick his head in your window trying to smell for alcohol, and waving his flashlight around looking for any reason to hold you.

Another tip I have is to refuse any sort of search, refuse field sobriety tests (the one legged stand, walk-and-turn, and the horizontal gaze nystagmus test). They can't make you take them, it doesn't besmirch you to refuse them, and I can't remember a single case where an officer said that my client passed all these tests.

Another tip is, that if you do get arrested and they ask you take a breathalyzer, you get 20 minutes to contact an attorney and you should take advantage of that but you only get it if you ask for it.

The final tip would be not to waive your Miranda rights, the officer will normally give you a questionnaire asking things like "When was your last drink?," "How long ago were you under the influence?" "Are you under the influence", things like that. I would not answer those questions in line with your Miranda rights.

    (Attorney Justin Summary - St Louis, Missouri)

As long as you comply with the police they will probably cut you loose that evening and they are not going to make you spend the entire weekend or the evening in the county jail. If you cause the police problems in everything that they are doing and don't comply with their requirements then they can make life very miserable for you. They can put you into  county and they can hold you up to three days. Put you in the county jail then. So I recommend if you are going to comply with that then you are OK. The place to fight your DUI is not at, when you're getting pulled over. The place to fight it is in the court room. And that's why the courts are set up.

    (Attorney Marc Taiani - Pittsburgh, Pennsylvania)

Don't take them [the field sobriety tests]. You don't have to take them, and they are designed for failure. Field sobriety tests are what is known as 'dual attention tests' and so the police officer, while he's telling my client to pay attention to one thing, he's asking him to do something else.

    (Attorney Steve Litz - Monrovia, Indiana)

Since many of the lawyers interviewed seemed to agree that one should refuse all field sobriety tests, (NOT breath, blood or urine – aka "chemical" tests) how can you refuse these tests, yet still be cooperative with police?

WHAT IS THE BEST WAY TO REFUSE A FIELD SOBRIETY TEST?

I would recommend that anyone asked to do that test, kindly say 'Thanks, but no thanks, I do not wish to do that.'
(Attorney Brendan Kelly - Omaha, Nebraska)

Well you don't have to be nasty, and certainly you can say: Look, my lawyer advised me that I don't have to take these tests, I don't feel comfortable taking a DUI test, or a field sobriety test.
(Attorney Steve Litz - Monrovia, Indiana)

If I know I've probably had too much to drink and I'm probably in trouble, I'd say, 'Officer, I respectfully decline to do any field sobriety tests.' That's what I'd do.
(Attorney Aaron Bortel - San Francisco, California)

Is there anything you CAN do when asked to do a breathalyzer, give a urine sample, or take a blood test? (these are called chemical tests and depending on the state, there may be penalties for refusing [ex: losing your driver's license for a year], you may be forced to do them, or other legal consequences)

Are There Situations Where Taking a Blood Test Is a Good Idea?

Basically any time you have a lab test, you have more issues: everything has to be handled properly, there's a chain of custody that has to be established and it has to be handled in a very specific fashion as determined by the Ohio Department of Health. And the prosecution bears the burden to show that all those rigorous procedures have been followed so any time there's a blood or urine test involved, whether it be alcohol or drugs, it opens up the doors to a lot of the offenses and many times I am able to keep the tests out of evidence which gives the prosecution very little to go on.

(Attorney Dale Naticchia - Cleveland, Ohio)

Well in Florida, arresting officers can't draw blood unless there's been an accident that's involved death or serious bodily injury. There are some very minor exceptions, but that's the primary basis on which blood is drawn.

(Attorney Steve Tinsley - Orlando, Florida)

Well, that's an interesting question. What I always tell individuals who have perhaps consumed some type of drug is that it is critical that they at least have one beer and the reason that it's critical that they have one beer is that because when they take that breath test, if it shows up that there's no alcohol and you have consumed some drugs, they are going to take a blood test from you which will then show the presence of drugs. However, if you have taken some alcohol, you will get a very low reading and therefore, the suspicion of drugs in your system will be greatly reduced.

(Attorney Lawrence Wolf - Los Angeles, California)

Once you've been arrested and charged with DUI / DWI, some of the most important decisions you'll make will soon present themselves to you, such as:

Should you go to trial or plead guilty and "get it over with"?

If you're convicted, can you get a DUI off your record in the future?

How do you get your license back and how long will it take?

One of the first things you'll be confronted with when you consider the evidence for and against you in your DUI case is whether you should push for a trial, a plea, or try to settle the case.

What percentage of DUI cases go to trial?

I think you're going to find that on any of these cases, most of them do not go to trial. It's not a matter of the percentages, it's a matter more of the police report, it's a matter of the attorney's ability to represent his client effectively, and I think you're going to find that a good attorney that has a good case may not need to fight it at trial. They may be able to get the case handled well before that, they may be able to get it handled  *through negotiations, they may be able to get it handled through motions, so you may not have to go to trial to get it handled. At the same time, the cases that are just no good, they are just dog cases, you're not going to be able to win the case no matter what you do, and it doesn't matter how good the attorney is, those cases you're going to want to do what you can to mitigate the damages.*

(Attorney Josh Hale - San Diego, California)

For us, about 7% of the cases we handle go through a full-blown trial. There's lots of different things that can happen before getting to the full jury trial phase and that could include going to a motions hearing, maybe arguing that the stop was conducted illegally under the Fourth Amendment, or some other issue with the evidence that the prosecution wants to present has a problem.

So a much higher percentage I'd say have gone to motions hearings, but in terms of full-blown trial, it's about 7%..... It is relatively low, but it's a little higher than what the average is for most criminal cases. It also varies by jurisdiction here in Colorado as well, that's probably something else to note, not each jurisdiction here, and by jurisdiction we're talking about each county because a DUI is a charge that's going to occur in a county court setting – not each county handles them the same way.

So some counties seem to have higher thresholds for what's going to happen, how they're going to deal with it, some counties seem to be a little bit more lenient. So depending on that county, also depends whether or not on whether that case is going to go to trial, depending on whether we can work something out in terms of a plea agreement with the DA's office. So that's also something that's important to consider, is what county is your DUI going to be prosecuted in.

(Attorney Zach Westerfield - Denver, Colorado)

About 80% have settled out of court. The other 20% are cases that go to trial. Out of the 20% that go to trial, usually by the time we impanel the jury, and we let the prosecutor know that we're serious, a lot of times we can get an offer out of that. Out of the hardcore cases that do not change, we take them to trial and it normally lasts between 1-2 days.

(Attorney Fred Woods - Greenville, South Carolina)

Oh I would say that a significantly high percentage of cases end up being plead probably upwards of 90%.

You know if you go to trial DUIs are expensive and if a test is done properly – I can cross examine a police officer and make him look silly – but it's much more difficult to cross examine a machine.... I'm one of the few attorneys in the state that is actually licensed to do the same kind of field sobriety tests that the police give and so I've taken very lengthy and detailed courses on field sobriety test analysis, so that is actually a lot of fun for me.

I love going to trial, I get more money if we go to trial. But it's not about me getting more money it's about me doing what's in my client's best interest. And so if I think it's in my client's best interest to take the case to trial, if I think we can win, I'll let him know. The vast majority of cases we end up pleading out. (Attorney Steve Litz - Monrovia, Indiana)

... if you're talking about a case that is set for trial, goes to trial, and then goes to verdict, I would say less than 5% but if you're talking about cases that are just set for trial, I would say about a quarter of my cases are set for trial at one point. Keep in mind that just setting something for trial does not mean that it will go to trial... Typically, on a first time DUI case one of the best strategies is to set it for trial.

The reason being, most judges will not punish a first-time offender with no criminal history, so if you go to trial and you lose you are likely to get the same punishment as you would have if you had pled guilty earlier, so for setting it for trial, you are pressuring the prosecutor to give you a good deal, and some of my best offers have come because I set something for trial.

(Attorney Jeff Yeh - Los Angeles, California)

Typically, on a first time DUI case one of the best strategies is to set it for trial. The reason being, most judges will not punish a first-time offender with no criminal history, so if you go to trial and you lose you are likely to get the same punishment as you would have if you had pled guilty earlier, so for setting it for trial, you are pressuring the prosecutor to give you a good deal, and some of my best offers have come because I set something for trial.

(Attorney Michael Tillotson - Virginia Beach, Virginia)

..the overwhelming majority of cases resolve themselves before going to trial. The way I structure my practice is to include going to trial. I work for a flat fee, so I tell people the upfront costs, and then there's additional fees if we need to hire experts in order to take the matter to trial. Probably 97% are resolved prior to trial either through motions or because the facts of the case are such that it's better to do a plea-bargain before going to trial.

(Attorney Brendan Kelly, - Omaha, Nebraska)

IS IT BETTER TO GO TO TRIAL, PLEAD, OR SETTLE A DUI CASE?

..it depends on what's at stake. As I said before, I've had a couple of clients who were pilots where if they lost their license they would have an inability to work for at least a year. That's a long time. And when the stake are that high I think it's smart to go to trial or get something reduced, whether that's the charging code, or sometimes I've been able to get them

charged with a different crime so they get a different set of penalties that they wouldn't have had otherwise.

It really depends on what the stakes are, because when you go to trial it costs a lot of money, and that's not just for the attorney, it costs a lot money through and through, and it's a gamble, you're not necessarily going to win, you're not necessarily going to lose at trial. It's a roll of the dice.
(Attorney Joshua Hale - San Diego, California)

Well what I tell my clients is, if you get offered something better than what you could get at trial, you need to consider the offer.

And if you're offered something much better than what you could get at trial, then you need to be real cognizant of that offer. You want to avoid trial if the damages could be great.
(Attorney Ken Stover - Reno, Nevada)

It really depends on the specific facts and evidence in the case. If you have what I call a valid legal or factual issue then it may very well be worth it to take it to trial. However, you need to consider the fact that in general juries are very, very negatively predisposed towards DUI cases, so you really need to have something solid. If you do not have something solid, it's better to use that as leverage to negotiate a better deal than to go trial.
(Attorney Anthony Lowenstein - San Francisco, California)

CAN A DUI CONVICTION BE EXPUNGED? (REMOVED, SEALED, OR DELETED FROM YOUR RECORD)

Missouri has its DUI Expungement Statute, but it's not easy to get. You've got to wait ten years. It can only be one DUI that you can expunge, the first one, you cannot have any alcohol-related incidents in those ten years that you're waiting to get it expunged, and you can't have a commercial driver's license.

(Attorney Justin Summary - St Louis, Missouri)

I really try to identify with the individual, and explain to them that although this seems like a nightmare that has befallen them, in fact this is something that we can get them out of, and get their license back, and have them move on with a good lesson in no time at all. And I try to make it as seamless as possible, where the person gets the maximum amount of the lesson, with the minimum amount of negative consequences, and I get them out of it in the fastest time possible. I also emphasize to my clients that as soon as possible after the DUI I like to help them expunge and clear their criminal record so that they have a clean slate.

(Attorney Anthony Lowenstein - San Francisco, California)

A lot of things that clients will call me for are expungements, where we will get the conviction dismissed even before probation is over or sometimes once probation is over. And that helps clean up the record.

 (Attorney Aaron Bortel - San Francisco, California)

It's important to know that you're not alone (approximately 1.5 million people each year are charged with some form of driving under the influence) and hearing what many people go through emotionally, socially, and financially when dealing with a DUI arrest and criminal investigation might provide some comfort and understanding.

WHAT ASPECTS OF A DUI DO PEOPLE HAVE THE MOST EMOTIONAL DIFFICULTIES DEALING WITH?

I would say for the most part, the criminal side of the DWI laws are fair. My main problem is the administrative side of DUI. To take someone's license away for a year for refusing a breath-test may be OK for someone like me who lives and works in Saint Louis and has access to public transportation, but most of Missouri's rural areas where public transportation is essentially non-existent means that you are essentially taking away someone's life for a year and their ability to make money and put food on the table for their family is too harsh and needs to be looked at.

 (Attorney Justin Summary - Saint Louis, Missouri)

[The loss of your license]...and driving on a DUI suspended license in some instances is harsher than the actual DUI. ....

Give an example if you are first time DUI violator and you don't have any prior conviction, you are eligible for a first time offender program. That offender program is anywhere from 6 months probation to 12 months probation, no jail time. And in most instances it's a 30-60 day license suspension. If you are driving during that time of suspended license and you get caught it's 60 -90 days in jail. $500 to a thousand dollar fine. And most importantly another 12 month license suspension. So that's where they really get you. It's not the original violation that gets you in trouble it's the subsequent one that causes problems.

(Attorney Marc Taiani - Pittsburgh, Pennsylvania)

I would say the license suspension tends to be the most alarming to people not to say that jail time and community service isn't a deterrent as well. A lot of people absolutely need to drive for work or for family or both, and their license being suspended for any period seems horrific to them, and that seems to be the largest consequence.

(Attorney Anthony Lowenstein - San Francisco, California)

I think you have the shame, a lot of people don't ever want to tell anyone that they were charged with a DUI or that they were convicted of a DUI. The sad part about that is, that if you really look at the numbers, probably one of your friends, or maybe someone reading this interview right now, they've been charged with a DUI and it's not an uncommon charge. I think that that's one of the big fears is how is everyone else going to look at you when all is said and done. I think the other thing is, it just costs a lot of money.

People are having a hard time, the economy right now is just tough and they're spitting out a lot of money, whether it's for the attorneys, whether it's for the court fees, the fines, the classes, and it ends up being a lot of money. And that's a source of fear too because jobs can be hard to come by.

Interestingly enough most people are concerned with their drivers license rather than are they going to go to jail... But they have to understand that it is a crime....It's not just a traffic ticket. You are going to be going to court. It is a crime.

Although the majority of the people, especially first time offenders will not be going to jail. It doesn't mean you can't. But they should treat it very seriously and make sure that they do everything that their attorney tells them to do. And they should obviously seek an attorney as quick as possible.

(Attorney Eric Sachs – Long Island, New York)

You may definitely feel that the punishments for "just having two beers" are extremely unfair and harsh, but you might be surprised to learn how DUI lawyers feel about the punishments…

ARE CURRENT DUI LAWS TOO HARSH?

Well DWI's and DUI's are serious problems in all of the United States. Recently over the last five years or so they have lowered the legal limit from .10 to .08. So it's hard for me say whether or not the penalties are too hard or too lax. ...What I will say that the people who do get arrested or charges with a DUI or a DWI in both New York and New Jersey are facing a serious consequence for their case, and they should seek competent council.

(Attorney Carl Spector - Fair Lawn, New Jersey)

I definitely feel that the current DUI punishments are too harsh. Keep in mind that in the 1970s that DUI used to be a traffic ticket, and over the years it's gotten harsher and harsher. And it seems to be a one-way street unfortunately. I think a lot of it is because it's political, you don't want to be the legislator who just made DUI laws more lenient. You always want to be the one to say, "I just signed this law, it's tougher now on DUI." So unfortunately, it's going to continue, and every year that I've practiced, it's gotten worse.

(Attorney Jeff Yeh - Los Angeles, California)

They are much too harsh. When I started practicing, as I said almost 15 years ago, drunk driving offenses were treated quite lightly in this state. I regularly would see people with third, fourth, fifth and sixth offenses. We didn't have the felony statute back then which made on the third offense it made drunk driving a felony. These people had no real incentive to improve their behaviors because it was still a misdemeanor *unless there was death involved ... or serious bodily injury in a traffic accident.*

But five years into my practice, Michigan had enacted a law [that] said if you have three drunk driving charges in ten years that would be a felony.

That is severe, I think. I don't know that a third offense really warrants it but in ten years its certainly understandable. Now 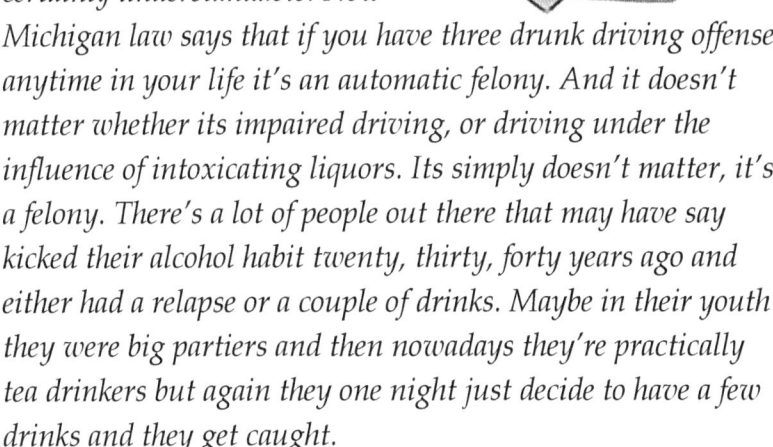 *Michigan law says that if you have three drunk driving offense anytime in your life it's an automatic felony. And it doesn't matter whether its impaired driving, or driving under the influence of intoxicating liquors. Its simply doesn't matter, it's a felony. There's a lot of people out there that may have say kicked their alcohol habit twenty, thirty, forty years ago and either had a relapse or a couple of drinks. Maybe in their youth they were big partiers and then nowadays they're practically tea drinkers but again they one night just decide to have a few drinks and they get caught.*

This is extraordinarily harsh treatment and I think that the pendulum has swung way too far on the criminal conviction side as opposed to the moderation position. Like I said, when I started practicing it was probably a little too lax. But now the pendulum has swung way over to the other side. There has been a lot of overreaction in my opinion by the state legislature. It's not to say that drinking and driving is appropriate, it isn't.

But [for] many people, jailing these individuals is not necessarily the best result because most of these people if you get them away from alcohol they are nice, ordinary individuals who hold a living, work, go home kiss their kids, treat them well and only when they get to alcohol do they have a problem and then of course [they] get behind a wheel. ... Now then again, these individuals also need that treatment [that] they have to be willing to accept. If they are not willing to accept it what does one do with them. Is jail or prison the answer?

I really don't know. That's up for obviously legislature to decide. So far they are deciding that these people need to be in jail. I just think that's there's got to be some solution in between. Whether that's the breath interlock device or an alcohol tether or something of that affect. Jail just seems to be, especially drunk driving law where we now have the super drunk driving law where any three in your life is a penalty just seems to be way over the top.

(Attorney Stuart Collis - Ypsilanti, Michigan)

....honestly given the crime and the possibility of what can occur while you are driving while you are intoxicated I think they are fair. The one thing that I think is unfortunate is that license suspension can happen. More people get in trouble for subsequent violations of driving on a DUI suspended license than they do on the DUI itself. And once you lose your driving license your whole life can fall apart.

You can't keep a job, you can't drive to work. You can't pay your bills and this causes you [to go] into basically a spiral [and that] causes you more problems that it is worth. So as it relates to the criminal sanctions they are not as harsh as it could be, as it is in some states. They are relatively fair. The problems that I have are the significant license suspension issues.

(Attorney Marc Taiani - Pittsburgh, Pennsylvania)

I think the current punishments at least in New York State, are too harsh. Again we are talking with people who have committed not a crime but a mistake. And it is fair for somebody who makes a mistake to possibly lose their jobs to lose their earnings? I think that's harsh. Does everybody need to have an Intoxilock device to take a breathalyzer every time they get into a car just because they were coming home from their child's wedding and this is the one time they have had a problem? I don't think so.

Certainly repeat offenders need to be dealt with, but even repeat offenders who are sick can.... You know, alcoholism is a disease. It's being sick. It's not a crime to be sick. They wouldn't put you in jail if you kept getting pneumonia or the flu. But if you can't beat your alcoholism and your addiction, they are going to put you in jail. I think that is ridiculous. I think that these people really need to be in a rehabilitation.

They need how to deal with their alcoholism not to be off the streets for 6 months or a year or even more and then be released back into society still without having the help as to how to handle whatever the trigger was that made them drink in the first place. The punishment in DWI cases definitely does not fit the crime.

(Attorney Eric Sachs - Bellmore, New York)

I would say it depends on what part of it we're looking at. Having to go to school, you know, it's not fun for anybody. The school themselves, there's a lot of good stuff you get out of the school. The length of the school makes that much of a difference. Some counties are too harsh. Others aren't. Some counties need to look at different levels of DUIs. For instance, Marin County will not allow negotiating for a wet or a dry reckless.

That's ridiculous. They end up having too many cases go to trial because of that, and it costs tax payers way to much money to do these trials.

They should have different levels. You've got all these strict penalties, and then on the license, though you can't drive for 30 days, they'll let you get a restricted license. That restriction is too strict. People, they're going to be on a restricted license. You need to allow more than what it does. It allows to and from work while you're working, and to and from your DUI school. Yet I have clients calling me up saying, wait, I need to get my kids to school, and that's not allowed. I need to go the doctors, I need to go to my therapist, I need to go to school, that's not allowed.

The Sacramento DMV which controls this says there are no excuses, there's no loop holes, and that's wrong. They need to be able to expand that restriction. It's really hurting people, and there's absolutely no reason to. Someone on a restricted license should be able to do whatever they want, except things like going out and drinking, and if you want to set up a time limit on a restricted license, that might be okay, but I think what's going to happen eventually and they've done this in other states.

 (Attorney Aaron Bortel - San Francisco, California)

I don't have a problem with somebody going to jail if they were driving drunk and the police did their job. I think the people need a taste of it to see what's going to happen if they keep doing it. What I do have a problem with is a police officer who says that they saw a tail light out when my clients tail lights were working fine and the only reason they say that is because they followed him after he left the liquor store, and then they stop him, and they test him, and he tested over the limit. Then we fight like hell.

 (Attorney Steve Litz - Monrovia, Indiana)

I think that they are too harsh to the extent that they affect an individual's ability to really provide for his family. Even in a first DUI situation, an individual is looking at losing their license for thirty days. That is a significant period of time for someone who is trying to get to work, trying to support his family, trying to do what he needs to do....

That thirty days, I think, should not be required. That individual certainly gets the message by the fines that are being imposed, the often six month to nine month alcohol program that they have to participate in, the restriction on their license; those are all messages enough. I don't think the additional message of having to lose your job and unfortunately, not provide for your family is necessary.

 (Attorney Lawrence Wolf - Los Angeles, California)

That's an interesting question. I think it depends on your perspective. I probably would say that I think that the majority of individuals who are charged with an OVI have learned their lesson tenfold by the time that they call their wife or girlfriend or parents to come and pick them up at the police station. And then to make them come back and have them deal with a suspended driver's license and possibly going to jail and doing all this stuff...That's a pretty significant punishment when you're talking about other crimes that, in my opinion, can be more serious than that, such as domestic violence or stealing or breaking into people's property.

There's no requirement that they have to go to a program or counseling or have your driver's license suspended for that even though they are arguably more serious.

(Attorney Doug Riddell - Columbus, Ohio)

I think I'm going to back off from that question a little bit, and the reason is there's a reason why it's against the law, and I think we all understand that. I think the problem is not whether the punishments are too lax or too stringent, or whether they are somewhere in between, I think the problem is the way we charge DUIs, you have people that may not be under the influence at a .08 blood alcohol level.

They may not have had any bad driving, they may not have had said anything wrong, they may have passed all their tests with flying colors, and they are still being convicted. I think the problem is that in some places we have prosecutors that are trying to find justice, my feeling that is in California in particular, prosecutors are trying to get convictions. They are not trying to find out whether the person was actually driving under the influence, they are just saying "Hey, tough luck Charlie" and I think that that's a big problem, more so on whether the punishments are too harsh. The punishments may be just right so long as we are convicting the right people.

                    (Attorney Joshua Hale - San Diego, California)

As a defense lawyer, I would like to say that the reason I fight them is because they are too harsh, but in fact it is a reality statistic that more people die in the United States every year due to alcohol-related traffic accidents, than in both Iraq and Afghanistan combined. So the police are getting tired of basically peeling bodies of the roads that were hurt because of drunk-driving. So most people can understand why drunk-driving really is a threat to human safety and life, so I don't think the punishments are too harsh...I think that there needs to be a set up that really deters people from drinking and driving and putting that risk to human life.

That being said, when I deal with clients one-on-one and I see that person as an individual is not a threat to society, can learn to be a safe driver and safe person, then that's my greatest joy as a lawyer is to help them navigate and make their way out of the system.

                    (Attorney Anthony Lowenstein - San Francisco, California)

Well I think, first of all, that that there has to be laws against drunk driving because people driving drunk on the roads is going to cause a lot of misery, death and injury. So there has to be some laws but one of the bad aspects of an OVI is that it stays on your record 50years and you can never seal it in Ohio. I think that that's very unfair.

In other states such as Pennsylvania, you can have the first one taken off your record. With communications science the way it is now, if any employer gets a background check on you and you have an OVI, it's going to show up and they keep it on your record for fifty years. I think that that's terrible. I think the restricted plates are terrible, I think they interfere with people working and it serves no good purpose. I wish that the system would be more serious about screening people that need treatment, need help, instead of punishment.... Otherwise these people, it doesn't matter what the punishment is, they're going to go out there and they're going to do it over and over again whether or not they have a license.

(Attorney Dale Naticchia - Cleveland, Ohio)

I don't know. Get back to me after someone's driven over one of my children or driven over one of my friends on a 3rd time DUI. I drive on the roads every day and I'm depending on other people to drive in a predictable manner and not kill me. The reason why the DUI punishments are so stiff is because for a long time you could kill people with cars and DUIs and get away with it and do minor punishment and be out drinking and driving in a short period of time later.

Alcohol is a dangerous drug, and when people drive on it the consequences are brutal. So on one hand, I see people who are never going to make this mistake again, they come into my office and they are mortified beyond reason.

And even if they're innocent, they're going to say "He smelled alcohol on my breath, I put myself in a situation where the officer could at least think I was DUI even when I'm not." And when they hear about the attorney's fees are, and the punishments are, and what the administrative consequences are, they look you right in the eye and say, "this aint never going to be a problem again" because they are smart people and they don't want to go through this again.

(Attorney Steve Tinsley - Orlando, Florida)

I think it's a difficult question to answer. I think that for most people that receive a first DUI arrest, they're going to think that the punishment is pretty harsh. By the time you pay it, get arrested, pay an attorney, go to court, have to go back to jail to finish out your jail sentence, have to pay court costs, do DUI school, do community service, do drug and alcohol evaluation and treatment and face the driver's license suspension; you've gone through a lot of punishment and you've spent a lot of money and dealt with a lot of stress and spent a lot of time dealing with it so it can be a harsh punishment for first DUI...But with that being said, we see so many second and third and fourth DUI arrests that obviously that punishment wasn't enough because it didn't stop people from continuing to go out driving while intoxicated.

(Attorney Kavan Grover - Atlanta, Georgia)

Besides the fear of the unknown after being charged with DUI, the question comes to mind:

Should you hire a DUI lawyer to defend your case or get a "free" public defender?

What about "just pleading guilty and getting it over with?"

How much does it cost, in total to defend yourself? (trial vs. no trial, plea agreement, 1st time DUI vs. 2nd, 3rd or 4th DUI)

How Much Does A DUI Cost?

Well with my firm, if you take a case all the way to from arraignment to jury trial, it will run you about $6,000 and that would be a first-time offense. Now keep in mind that not all the cases have to go to trial, and without trial it would be significantly cheaper.

But if you had a 2nd or 3rd DUI, or an accident or some unusual, aggravated set of circumstances, it could run you higher. If somebody wants me to set something for trial, then I still have to prep for trial, even if it doesn't end up actually going to trial. A lot of times in LA County we can get deals without having to go to trial, and that would run you about $2,000.

(Attorney Jeff Yeh - Los Angeles, California)

It varies, but generally it's between $2,000 and $10,000. At our firm we have flat fees depending on your situation, depending on what you blow. So for example, let's say that you blow a .08, which is the legal limit, the flat fee is $2,000. If you blow a .13 as your DUI First, this is DUI First I'm talking about, it's generally about $3,000 just for the attorney's fee. If you have a DUI Second and it's between .08 and .15, that's another level, DUI Third is another level, on up to where you have a DUI Fourth, it's going to be about a $10,000 case.

(Attorney Fred Woods - Greenville, South Carolina)

Misdemeanor DUIs locally will be $1,500 and that includes the DMV hearing that I'd necessarily use to ask those questions that I want the answers to. I don't get all my answers from the police reports, I need to understand what this police officer did and how he did it, clearly by how he was trained to do it.

And if he wasn't trained properly, then he probably didn't do it properly, and there may be a lot of defensible issues in the DUI itself.

If it's a felony, it runs $3,500 to start the case, if we went to jury trial, it would be much more than that. And if we're dealing with felony death cases, it would be much higher than that. That would depend on the individual circumstances.

(Attorney Ken Stover - Reno, Nevada)

It kind of depends upon the situation. The way our law firm does it is by giving people the option to pay by the hour or working on a flat fee, and each circumstance is going to be a little bit different depending upon the seriousness of the charge,

 how many prior offenses that person has, are they charged with DWAI, are they charged with DUI, what type of tests did they do, there's all kinds of factors, so it's going to vary, the costs are going to vary. But I would say on average you are going to be looking at legal expenses of at least $2,500, and if you go to trial you're going to be looking at more than that, and then you're going to be looking at additional expenses.

 You're going to be looking at $1,000-$2,000 in court costs and fines, you're going to have to pay increased insurance rates for having to carry SR-22 insurance, as well as having a major traffic violation on your record, you're looking at having to do DUI classes, what they call level 2 alcohol education, and possibly therapy, here in Colorado, and those things run about $15 or so per hour and usually you're looking at a minimum of 24 hours, all the way up to 96 hours if you have to do a lot of therapy, that can get expensive. You're looking at having to do community service and pay fees and bonds for that, you're also looking at some other incidental expenses that you're going to have to run into.

 One of the conditions may be some kind of sobriety monitor either while you're on bond, while your case is pending, or it may be a condition of probation if you receive, so you may have to do random breath tests, or urine analysis tests, or maybe have to do something more serious, like a SCRAM device, or get the interlock device installed in your vehicle, that costs money to install, there's a monthly rental fee, the cost to uninstall, so the costs can spiral upwards.

So the cost of a DUI from what I've seen, including legal fees, can run upwards of $10,000.

(Attorney Zach Westerfield - Denver, Colorado)

I'd say the ballpark pre-trial cost would be somewhere between $4,000 and $7,500. You've go to look at it just as plain old time. An attorney charges anywhere from $250 to $400 an hour on average, and if someone is charging say $300 and the cost is $4,000, then that's around 12-13 hours. That's not a whole lot of time on a case, but it is enough time to work and fight a case up to trial. On the other side, after you get to the point where you're going to trial,

you're looking probably at around $2,500 to $5,000 for every day of trial. These trials can last anywhere from a couple of days up to a week, I would say most last 2-3 days, and I would say a fair charge for that would be $2,500 - $4,500 a day.

I'm somewhere right in the middle of that. You've also got to pay for a forensic toxicologist too, and a good forensic toxicologist costs several thousand dollars to testify, and they've got to look at the blood and breath,

so because of that you're going to looking at a lot of money both before and during trial. That's why I was saying you have to look at what's at risk whether or not you should go to trial, because with most of these cases it costs a lot of money to go trial, and the results may not be any better when all is said and done.

(Attorney Joshua Hale - San Diego, California)

If you're going to spend money and hire a DUI attorney, then you'll surely find it helpful to understand what professional representation can bring to the table vs. trying to defend yourself or using the public defender's office...

WHAT ARE THE ADVANTAGES OF HIRING A DUI ATTORNEY?

Let me just begin by talking about the underlying charge. If we can get the DUI knocked down to any kind of reckless driving charge, then there wouldn't be any of the DMV consequences from the court. In other words, you will not face a license suspension from court, and that's important to a lot of people. And in getting it reduced it means you have reckless driving, or speeding, or something that's not a DUI on your record, which could help you when you apply for job or two a school, or whoever looks at your record. And the second thing is we can obviously help people with their licenses. If you request a hearing within ten days, and request a stay of suspension, your license will be valid pending the entire DMV process which could drag on for 6 months easily, so you want to be able to drive while this thing is pending. Most people don't know that, they let the ten days slip and then they lose their license. The third thing is jail. We could reduce jail or eliminate jail, or convert it to something else, for example, home confinement, electronic bracelet, or community service.

The final thing is we can get you into a lesser program, or eliminate the alcohol program altogether. These programs can last up to 32 months, so obviously you want to do as short a program as you can or no program at all, and most people don't realize that even if you get the charge reduced just a little bit, to reckless driving for example, you don't have to do a program, it's not a legal requirement

(Attorney Jeff Yeh - Los Angeles, California)

We try to keep our clients ability to drive. The laws are consistently changing, the burdens keep changing, and it's really upon us to fight for our client. But the things we do, are trying to get the charges reduced, trying to get the whole thing dismissed is really the goal. The service I provide includes initially when they get the ticket all the way up to a trial.

So for instance, we have a law that says you only have ten days from receiving the ticket to try to petition to keep your driver's license or it will automatically be taken for a minimum of 90 days. So we step in right away to try to stop the client's license being revoked, and carefully examine the facts of the case and try to do everything possible to ensure that you are not convicted.

(Attorney Brendan Kelly - Omaha, Nebraska)

This is an individualized question and that is attorney-speak for wiggle room, lots of attorneys don't want to answer that, but the truth is, every case is different. That being said, when there is something that I'm able to do, let's say reduced jail time, reduced fines, reduce the amount of time that you don't have a license, if there's other charges, reduce the amount of time that you're going to jail for the other charges, if that ends up being the case.

Yes, that happens pretty frequently, I hate to say that happens one in two, or two in three, it's a very individualized matter. With that being said, my office's ability to have charges reduced, or jail time reduced, or something done for my client, is pretty strong, I can't say that it's 100% obviously but I would that either through skill or luck, I have had pretty good results for my clients.

(Attorney Joshua Hale - San Diego, California)

There are some cases you get where you really don't have any good defense and the person gave the police officer a lot of evidence against them and took the breath test or took the blood test and had a high Blood Alcohol Content or had illegal drugs in their system. Sometimes there's just cases that are hard to defend and hard to get any type of reduction but I'd say, in terms of the cases where the person does have a good legal defense, we're highly successful in getting the consequences of the charge reduced if not dismissed.

When we take a case on, we do a full investigation and we immediately request the police report, we request any video that there is, we request the 911 call or CAD report regarding the case, we request the officer's post records to see what type of training they have. If it's a breath test case, we request the records regarding the Intoxilyzer 5000 to see if its had any problems, to see if it was calibrated correctly.

If it's a drug test, we take the time to call the lab and discuss the results with the person who did the test. So when you have a private attorney, if you have a good attorney that does the right investigation, you're going to get everything done properly and quickly. I would never recommend representing yourself on one of these cases, there's just, the law's just too complex; there's a lot of science behind DUI law.

(Attorney Kavan Grover - Atlanta, Georgia)

I think, probably, the most beneficial thing is us being able to assist those people who perhaps do have some problem with drugs or alcohol and this perhaps is a wakeup call; being able to assist those clients in getting, perhaps, the assistance they need with those issues.

(Attorney Lawrence Wolf - Los Angeles, California)

Well, when I meet with a client, in the vast majority of DUI cases, 95% of them or better, there are two cases pending against a person. One is the criminal case, state of Florida, jail time driver's license suspension, community service, significant fines, that sort of thing.

The other case is the administrative driver's license suspension and your DUI ticket, in the majority of cases is a temporary driver's license that's only good for ten days. That ticket says that if you want to challenge that driver's license suspension you have to challenge it and apply for a formal review within ten days of receiving the ticket.

When someone comes to my office to meet with me, I keep the forms in my office, even if they don't hire me, I help them fill out the forms, tell them what they've got to do, where they've got to apply for the review if they're going to get the money together to try to hire a lawyer. But that process of applying for a review also causes the majority of people to receive another temporary driver's license, good for business purposes only, it's good for another 42 days.

So the client comes in to see me, first thing we do is try to figure out when he was arrested, is he eligible for a permit almost always that's the case, and so we calculate the ten days from his arrest up until how long he can drive on the ticket, then we arrange for him to deliver the papers he needs to the DMV so that just prior to the ten days of driving on his ticket,

he gets another license good for 42 days...And during that course of the 50 or 51 day time period, we get paperwork together to find out what we can do to save the driver's license.

(Attorney Steve Tinsley - Orlando, Florida)

Well the number one way in which I can help someone is, in most of DUI cases I handle, I either completely prevent or drastically reduce any time that they spend in jail. Right now I'm referring to first-time DUIs. Multiple DUIs are in a different category, but for most, over 90% of the cases I get are first DUIs. And for first-time DUIs, I can prevent completely or drastically minimize the amount of jail time granted. The other thing I can prevent or minimize is the duration of license suspension. So while I may not be able to make a DUI go away where there's valid evidence for it, I can often negotiate it down to a form of reckless driving or at least completely minimize the consequences to the statutory minimums. That's the way that I or a good lawyer can add value to a client versus them representing themselves.

(Attorney Anthony Lowenstein - San Francisco, California)

Reduction or elimination of jail time, reduction of fines and fees, entering into the diversion program or state detention, and the state initially says 'no way' and we have a hearing and the judge overrules that decision, so that's great. Reduction of suspension of your driving privilege is a huge benefit, especially if you are commuting to work – so we can certainly help you with that.

And also, what I like to pride myself on is my practice, is that I'm with my clients from soon after the moment of arrest, to requesting all the necessary hearings that we need to request, getting ready for first court appearances, discovery, requesting facts of discovery, all the way from the initial point, throughout the entire court procedure, after you enter into treatment, keeping in touch with you while you are in treatment, so that you are on good terms with people that are providing the treatment, all the way to getting the sentence or the result.

(Attorney Shannon Wilson - Portland, Oregon)

Well first of all, obviously, I have a generally a greater understanding of law than your average, ordinary individual.

This is what I went to law school for, this is what I studied, this is what I practice on a daily basis. So I'm going to be able to make sure they have their constitutional rights protected, I'm going to be able to make sure that the police followed all the correct procedures, that they made sure their their data master was properly calibrated, that they had fulfilled their fifteen minute waiting requirement before the breath test was given so that there was no foreign objects put in the mouth, etc, which might skew the results which might make them invalid. So I'm going to be able to serve first of all as a double check on all the constitutional rights as well as the administrative procedures required to be followed every time that there is a breath alcohol device test done. Secondly,.

What I'm going to be able to do is I'm going to be able to negotiate with the prosecuting attorney whoever it may be, whatever county, city, or state to get the best possible result if this is just a plea situation. If it is not a plea situation I can bring a motion to the court for reasons why evidence must be suppressed or why the case must be dismissed prior to getting to a trial.

And if it gets to a trial obviously I have connections with the appropriate expert witnesses to bring them in to testify as to why certain things are not as obvious as they might seem or as presented by a prosecuting attorney.
(Attorney Stuart Collis - Ypsilanti, Michigan)

Well most important things since the DUI laws in Pennsylvania have mandatory sentencing, if somebody promises you oh I can get you stuff that no one else can, that's a fallacy. In Pennsylvania it is basically mandatory sentencing means based on your blood alcohol level or your DAC level it is going to put you in a certain guideline range.

And then basically based on which county you are in it is going to be up to the district attorney whether or not you have or if they make available to you electronic monitoring. What we do at attorneys at law at my office, we walk you through the process explain to you the process so you know what's going to happen. We explain to you what your court appearance is going to be like. We take you there. We make sure you we get you the best possible deal that we possibly can.
(Attorney Marc Taiani - Pittsburgh, Pennsylvania)

I think that's probably what everybody wants to know, when they're picking up the phone or emailing a lawyer, what can they expect from a lawyer. What I provide quite frankly is a number of things, first education as we talked about earlier in the day and secondly to try to minimize whatever penalties may occur. The first approach would be to try to get the case dismissed or to try the case and try to get a not guilty verdict.

Short of that if we are not going to have a trial, we try to, in New York we try to get it reduced to driving while ability is impaired (DWAI) which is not a crime but a traffic infraction which reduces your suspension time down to 90 days as opposed to 6 months and also reduces the fines and it also eliminates the need for an interlock device. So that is a critical factor that everybody needs to understand, the lawyer can in the law minimize exposure by someone who has been accused of this offense if they go about it the right way.

(Attorney Carl Spector - Fair Lawn, New Jersey)

How Do You Get Suitable Legal Representation to Defend Your DUI?

It's real simple – talk. Talk to the attorney that you intend to hire, or talk to five attorneys. Talk to them and find out they are what they say they are. You want to know that this attorney is going to represent you to the best of his ability and that he's going to represent you strenuously. Ask questions of the attorney, and if he doesn't answer them in a satisfactory manner, go to the next guy.

(Attorney Joshua Hale - San Diego, California)

They have a nationwide system called Martindale-Hubbell that evaluates us, and I am evaluated as the highest of ethics and the highest of legal ability in the rating system. And I think that's important, that whoever anyone hires, that they hire someone who has that top rating. Because that indicates that they have that level of respect from fellow judges and lawyers that are needed to practice in whatever county you're in front of. You have to have that level of expertise and you have to have that level of respect to effectively practice.

(Attorney Michael Byrne - Chicago, Illinois)

There are a number of very good DUI lawyers in the San Francisco Bay area. You've got to find the right one for you. You've got to interview them. You've got to make sure who you talk to is the attorney who's going to defend you, and you really, really need to make sure that they know what they're doing. If you hire an attorney who has a big name, is part of a firm, they have a number of attorneys working for them, more than one or two. You're not going to know who the attorney is whose representing you every time. ...I always say talk to one or two attorneys at least before you make your decision because it's a big decision, and you'll make the right choice for you if you do that.

(Attorney Aaron Bortel - San Francisco, California)

[Look for] two things. Number one, they should always ask, who is the attorney that is actually going to represent me? Keep in mind that a common industry trick is to take your money, and then pass the case down to someone who is not experienced,

for example, the young associates, and every time you call, a different attorney will talk to you and a different attorney goes to court for you every time, depending on whose available at that given day. So you want to make sure that you have the person that you paid to represent you.

The second thing you should look for is, does this firm specialize in DUI? A lot of law firms out there will take whatever walks in the door; divorce, bankruptcy, personal injury, and DUI is just one of the many things that they do. DUI is a very complicated field as there are both criminal and civil consequences, so you owe it to yourself to have someone who specializes in it to represent you.

(Attorney Jeff Yeh - Los Angeles, California)

Remember, if you choose to hire an attorney, realize that they're a human being just like you, with their own reasons for agreeing to defend you. You should definitely feel like any attorney you choose respects you as a human being in return, and not just a paycheck.

Here's some insight of the actual people who have chosen to be DUI attorneys...

Why Do You Practice DUI Law?

DUI cases are very complicated. You're dealing a lot with science, with medical issues, and it's truly an area where innocent people can be convicted and the consequences are just so severe. It's an area that's very political and so the state is very eager to convict and they use machinery, the breath test machines that can be so variable and can give false results on people, but yet they want to make it sound like these things are perfect. So for me coming from a background that wanted to help people this was an area where I could help some people who were innocent fighting against the state that really wanted to convict them and wasn't concerned with false results and injustices and things like that.

And I know this is a long answer, I said it was, but one other thing is that the constitutional protections given to all of us, there's no other area of law, where those protections are being eroded as they are in DUI cases and that's a whole lengthy discussion but suffice it say that my colleagues in the National College have inspired me to try to be the very best attorney that I can be and I can do that representing those citizens that are accused of driving under the influence of alcohol.

(Attorney Michael Tillotson - Virginia Beach, Virginia)

Even before I started to become an attorney, I was always very interested in the criminal justice system. As an undergraduate I focused on criminal justice degree and when I entered law school, I knew that I was going to be focusing on getting experience and education in criminal justice.

So when I did graduate from Wilson Clark in 2005, I did receive a certificate in criminal law. And DUI defense work is just another branch of criminal work carried out here in Oregon. I really enjoy doing this type of work, and here in Oregan it's very complicated and there's a lot of changes in the law, recent changes actually, so it's a very exciting area to be working in legal defense at the moment.

(Attorney Shannon Wilson - Portland, Oregon)

In terms of just criminal defense work generally, I find the work challenging. I think it's a very useful function to perform, and gives me the opportunity to help. In terms of concentrating on drunk driving, it is an offence that covers the whole spectrum of people, from people with not much money to the people who are very wealthy financially, to men and women equally. So it's an offense that has very broad consequences for people, it affects their liberty in the worst case scenario and their driver's licenses, so it's the type of offense that can affect a lot of people with negative consequences and I can help minimize those consequences many times.

(Attorney John English - Lansing, Michigan)

We have OVIs here in Ohio, and I think for me as someone who considers myself a professional, it's amazing to me how there really is no, typical, prototypical defendant in a traffic DUI case,

so you're going to see a lot of people who have never been in trouble in their lives who are grandmothers, parents, professionals, executives, lawyers, stockbrokers, marketers, I mean, every level of person could go out, have a night out with friends or with family or a work function, and come home, have too much to drink and suddenly they're looking for an attorney, and that's kind of where I feel like I can help people, relate to them and kind of guide them through that process. For me, it's pretty rewarding. Especially because I know I can usually get a good result for my client.

(Attorney Doug Riddell - Columbus, Ohio)

As a criminal defense attorney, I find that I can be of great service to a lot of different type of people. The service essentially boils down to educate people so that they can take control of their case. When people get arrested they get a summons, they get in trouble, and they feel like they have no control. So what I try to do is to educate my clients so they can feel a sense of control. Then they can make really informed decisions based on the information and the education I provide to them.

With regard to the DWI's or DUI's, one of the reasons I like doing those cases is they are very complicated and very complex. There's a lot of science involved, there's a lot of law involved, there's a lot of rights to protect and I like to dig my teeth into those and really get down to where I can really protect my clients' rights and help them take a disposition that is most favorable to them, by exploring all of the avenues in the case.

(Attorney Carl Spector - Fair Lawn, New Jersey)

The criminal practice, practicing criminal law is very enjoyable for me because I get to go to court every single day. I meet clients, I do legal pleading. So it's a little bit of everything. So it;s very exciting also knowing that you are helping somebody out who is going through a very difficult time period in their life. And we try and work them and help them through their problems, alcohol related or whatever it is that led them to drink and to drive.

And you know we want to help them so that they don't lose their job, they don't lose their license and see what we can do to help them to move through and get through this difficult time in their life. In fact it is very enjoyable seeing that after it is resolved they are not really nailed to the cross if you will.

(Attorney Marc Taiani - Pittsburgh, Pennsylvania)

Well I have been a public servant most of my life. From the time that I was a kid, moving up to the time that I was the assistant district attorney. And then the time to become a criminal defense attorney. And I realized that there things that you need to do that are the right thing to do for people and people need help. They don't want to be preyed upon. They want to have somebody that knows the law and can help them with whatever problem they seem to have. DUI's DWI's have become such a major issue now a days that I find that people moreso than anything, the innocent people, the people that are not criminals. It's a mistake that you can make. Like a speeding ticket or anything else. It's a mistake but it can be a very costly mistake. And it can vastly and grossly effect your life.

(Attorney Eric Sachs – Long Island, New York)

WHAT'S THE MOST IMPORTANT THING YOU WANT TO SAY TO PEOPLE CHARGED WITH A DUI WHO READ THIS BOOK?

Kevin Leckerman, Esq.
(Philadelphia, Pennsylvania & Southern New Jersey)
You mentioned the word attack, and that's essentially how I approach these DWI cases, I don't sit back and defend a DWI charge, because frankly in New Jersey you're not going to get

anywhere if you're just sitting back and waiting for the prosecutor to hand you a deal.

Mark Taiani, Esq.
(Pittsburgh, Pennsylvania)

I've been practicing now a little over ten years and it actually all started when a couple of my good friends got pulled over by the police. I was just starting to get involved in criminal work. And they asked me hey Mark can you handle these cases so I said sure I'll give it a shot.

On a monthly basis to my knowledge in our office we normally do anywhere between 10 to 20 cases a month. And those all range from either being first time offenders to multiple offenders. I have represented people with as many as 8 DUI's.

Attorney Ken Stover (Reno, Nevada)

I had a lot of DUI prosecution experience. What I learned in that is that the law enforcement officers don't always understand how to get it done, so on the defense side of things it seemed an opportunity for me to go in and challenge how they were doing what they were doing, and it's been very successful.....I left prosecution in 2000 and have 15 year's experience on both sides of the aisle, it's been ten year's in defense.

Attorney Zach Westerfield (Denver, Colorado)

[DUI] is the most common thing that the average Joe citizen who isn't a felon or anything like that, is going to have to deal with, and the fact that it can affect your license, it can affect your job, it can affect your family, are all reasons that I decided to practice in that area. ...I try to deal with everybody on a very personalized, individual basis.

Anthony Lowenstein (San Francisco, California)
I really try to identify with the individual, and explain to them that although this seems like a nightmare that has befallen them, in fact this is something that we can get them out of, and get their license back, and have them move on with a good lesson in no time at all.

Justin Summary (Saint Louis, Missouri)
A happy client is your best advertising, and I try to keep that in mind when I'm taking on more...I didn't have my nose in a law book for three years to look at your file and plead you out. I did it to gain a knowledge on how to defend these types of cases, and defend your rights, and how to do it well.

Brendan Kelly (Omaha, Nebraska)
I've been an attorney for almost 20 years now and during that time I've probably handled 10,000 DUI cases. My practice focus has been on criminal defense, with an emphasis on DUI law because its an area where I felt the burdens on the people accused are pretty huge. It's not like in a normal criminal case where you have to have proof beyond a reasonable doubt in order for the prosecutor to get a conviction. In a DUI case, it's assumed that the defendant is guilty until proven otherwise.

Joshua Hale (San Diego, California)
We don't do only DUI .... DUI specialists, the way their certification works is that they can only handle DUI cases. So what happens if there's a case where there's a DUI, and you

happen to have your gun collection in the car or let's say you happen to have something that's illegal on top of the DUI, does that mean that they can't represent you, or does that mean that they're not going to be able to represent you to the best of their ability. ...it's not how many cases you've handled, so much as, do you have good results? My office has had very good results, whether it's luck or skill, we've had good results.

John English (Lansing, Michigan)
Our client's well being is our number one consideration. In these types of offenses (drinking and drugged driving offense) at least some people arrested for these types of charges do have issues related to alcohol abuse. If somebody has those types of problems who is one of our clients we assist them in getting any help that they need while at the same time aggressively defending their case.

Michael Byrne (Chicago, Illinois)
...to be a criminal defense attorney is what makes our country great. It separates our country from what we've seen go on in Northern Africa the last couple of months, where frequently you see a police state and people have no rights. In our country we have the right to due process, we have the right to a lawyer and we have the right to fair representation in a court. And without lawyers checking the police, police would get away with far more than they do... I found that over the last 30 years the pendulum with respect to DUIs has only swung one way.

The police are becoming increasingly aggressive at arresting people for DUI, whether it's the quotas they have or the counties making money from court appearances, but they seem to arrest anyone they can for DUIs – they seem to try to get a certain number of arrests. So I think it's important that aggressive criminal defense lawyers step in.

Shannon Wilson (Portland, Oregon)

What I like to pride myself on in my practice, is that I'm with my clients from soon after the moment of arrest, to requesting all the necessary hearings that we need to request, getting ready for first court appearances, discovery, requesting facts of discovery, all the way from the initial point, throughout the entire court procedure, after you enter into treatment, keeping in touch with you while you are in treatment, so that you are on good terms with people that are providing the treatment, all the way to getting the sentence or the result – I'm always available to my clients ...

because I really feel that part of being an attorney is not just the advocating portion of it, it's also the counseling portion of it, so that you as a client understand what the process is, what you are obligated to do – and I think that a lot of people feel that they are in more control of their lives to have someone in their corner in their case and ask questions at the right time.

Jeff Yeh, Esq.
(Los Angeles, California)

A lot of law firms out there will take whatever walks in the door; divorce, bankruptcy, personal injury, and DUI is just one of the many things that they do. DUI is a very complicated field as there are both criminal and civil consequences.... I focus, specialize and concentrate on DUI. You owe it to yourself to have a DUI specialist on your side.

Kavan Grover, Esq.
(Atlanta, Georgia)

When I originally went to law school, I was actually planning on being a patent attorney and I soon realized that it was not very interesting and not very rewarding.

With criminal law, you get to deal with regular people and despite the stigma that a lot of people have with criminal defense law, you know, pretty much everyone in society has the possibility of facing criminal charges and they have a very high chance of having a great impact on people's lives and I think it's really important for those people that they're well-represented.

Lawrence Wolf, Esq.
(Los Angeles, California)

Well, after thirty-five years of practicing criminal law, it's really the most exciting part of the law that I can tell, it's the type of situation where you can get immediate relief for the client, where you can get immediate results for a client. That is even more so true in the criminal justice system when dealing with DUIs. The way the law is in California is there's this now a 10 day requirement that you have to contact the DMV within, and so that really requires an immediate assistance to the unfortunate person whose been arrested for drunk driving.

Dale Naticchia, Esq.
(Cleveland, Ohio)

In the twenty-five years that I've been practicing, I've practiced in a lot of different areas of law including corporate law. But I like things on an individual basis and people that get involved in the criminal system have a real immediate need and to do something good for them, to help them through, they're very appreciative and that motivates me but OVIs especially and DUIs as they call them; they're people, they're very good people that have never been involved with the system before.

They either made a mistake of judgment or the officers made a mistake of judgment. They find themselves in a very bad situation and I can help them out and it always makes me feel good when they come out and they feel good about themselves and the result.

Doug Riddell, Esq.
(Dayton, Ohio)

I have handled thousands of OVI cases in my career, whether it was from the prosecutor's side of the defense side, so I've seen all the perspectives.

I know the parties and the relationships with the prosecutors and the judges that is going to be necessary to effectively advocate for you on a case. So I think it's important to have an attorney who's going to know the law, who's going to fight for you in the law, and is going to have good relationships with people to make sure that whatever deals or whatever possible options that are out there that we can take advantage of them.

Steve Litz, Esq.
(Monrovia, Indiana)

My approach to defending drunk driving cases has always been pretty straightforward, you know I examine the police report, we interview the officers, we interview everyone that does the testing, and then I advise my client on whether there are issues that need to be explored further. And if the police have done their job, and the test is accurate and the stop was valid and all of the other things that go into analyzing DUIs were done properly, then I try to work out the best deal I can for my client. I don't waste my clients' money. ....I never sugarcoat things with my clients and I have a reputation in this county and state-wide of fighting very hard for my clients.

Aaron Bortel, Esq.
(San Francisco, California)
I've always been interested in defending people charged with crimes. I knew going into law school and when I was an undergrad, I wanted to do criminal defense work, and instead of doing what a lot of other attorneys do – what civil attorneys do – which is a lot of fighting over money. I wanted to help people. And I can really help a lot of people when they're being charged by the government for committing a crime and something like DUI is something that most people who drive a car and drink alcohol can relate to.

Michael Tillotson, Esq.
(Virginia Beach, Virginia)
I started practicing 20 years ago and worked in a corporate law firm with 90 attorneys for two years handling business litigation and I was very unhappy doing that.

I always thought of myself as going to law school to help people so when I went into private practice after about two years on my own, I started doing criminal cases and personal injury cases. Through the years, I guess it was around 1998, is when I attended my first DUI seminar out in Las Vegas, a national DUI seminar.

So I'd been practicing for about 8 years handling DUI cases, and I realized after attending that first DUI seminar in Vegas, through the National College for DUI Defense, which I'm proud to be a member of and the state delegate for. When I attended that seminar I realized that I had no idea what I was doing in a DUI case.

Fred Woods, Esq.
(Greenville, South Carolina)
Ever since I was 9 years old, I knew I wanted to become a lawyer..... Being a lawyer was a way for me to help society in some way and also for me to be able to make a good living for myself and do something that I thought would be good for me and is respectable. In regards to DUI law, it is a subset of criminal law. I only practice two types of law, one being criminal law, the other being personal injury. Personal injury is usually auto-wrecks and accidents, things of that nature. Criminal law is murder cases on down to traffic tickets. A subset of criminal law is DUI law.

DUI law is the type of law that is best matched to my skills and abilities to be able to help people. It allows you to be able to do a large number of trials very quickly, it allows you to be able to interact with prosecutors, interact with juries and helps to get your name out there as well.

Steven R. Tinsley, Esq.
(Orlando, Florida)

On one hand, I'm located next to a liquor store so there's probably some serious irony there. On the other hand, I've been doing this for around 25 years. I've been defending people on DUIs for around 23 of them. I take this seriously. My job is to protect my client the best way I know how and to make sure they understand what it is that I'm going to try to accomplish for them, and to tell them to their face in no uncertain terms, in a manner in which they're not going to get confused later on where I think they stand.

Stuart Collis, Esq.
(Ypsilanti, Michigan)

My biggest concern in representing individuals and making sure their personal and constitutional rights are protected. When I was in law school that was one of the main things that I wanted to make sure was guaranteed because everyone has certain constitutional rights. And it is our job as a criminal attorney or even as a drunk driving attorney to make sure that those are protected. We set bounds and they need to be kept within them ....

In terms of what I do, I am very client oriented. I am here to service my client, I am here to help my client and help to each client is individual. Some people want to assert every single defense that there is out there and drag the state through the ringer.

Others are more content to say let's take our best stab at this and if it's not meant to be or the odds are not in our favor lets arrange something with the people. The key is, is that I am here to service the client, I'm here to accommodate my client and it's not the other way around.

My practice is about helping people, it is not about being the person who says you will do this.

Carl Spector, Esq.
(Fair Lawn, New Jersey & New York, New York)
I find that a lot of people simply don't understand their rights, and with a little bit of information from me and some education from me they can take back the control that they lose by being arrested and not being able to make a really informed decision when it comes time to making an important decision in your case.

Richard Jacobs
Speakeasy Marketing, Inc.
73-03 Bell Blvd #10
Oakland Gardens, N.Y. 11364
(888) 225-8594

www.ingramcontent.com/pod-product-compliance
Lightning Source LLC
Chambersburg PA
CBHW061514180526
45171CB00001B/180